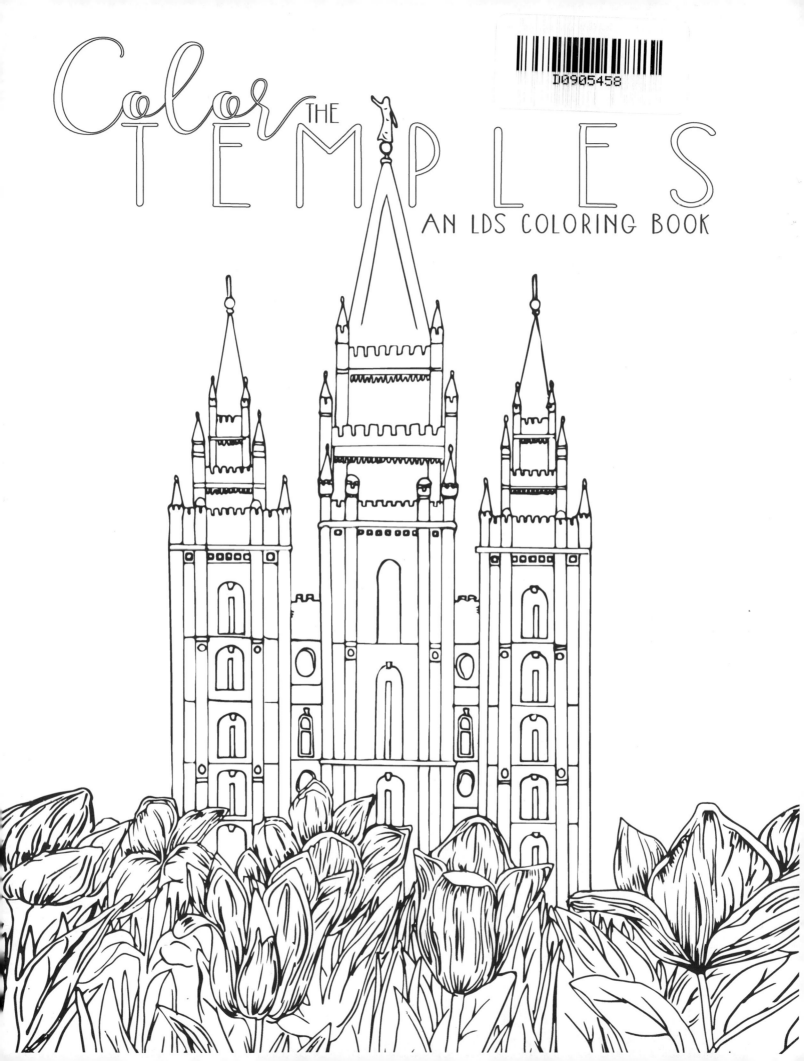

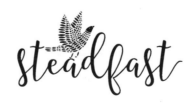

@STEADFAST_CREATIVES

Follow us on Instagram!

TEMPLES ARE A PLACE OF PEACE.

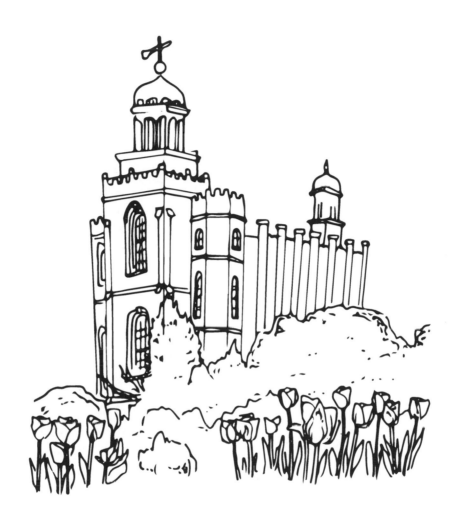

They uplift us and are a safe haven from the world. As we ponder and draw closer to them, our lives are enriched. Please enjoy this coloring book meant to inspire and truly turn our minds and hearts toward the temple and God.

Malachi 4:6

and he shall
turn the
heart
of the fathers
to the children,
and the heart
of the children
to their fathers

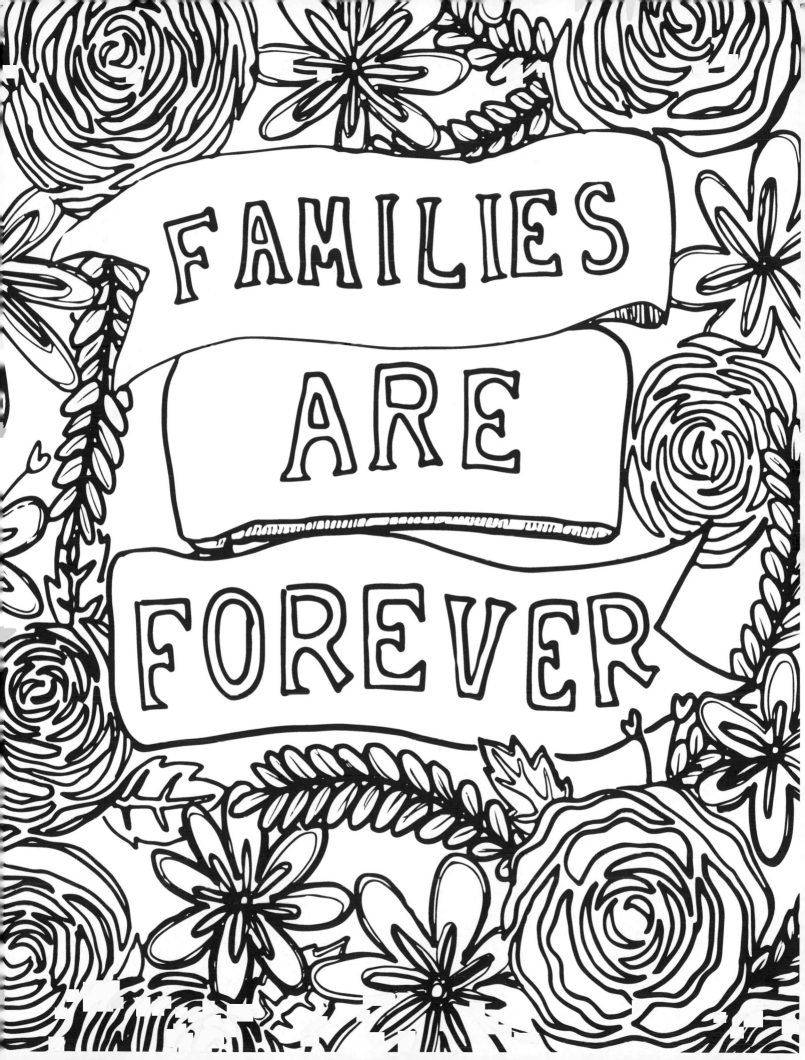

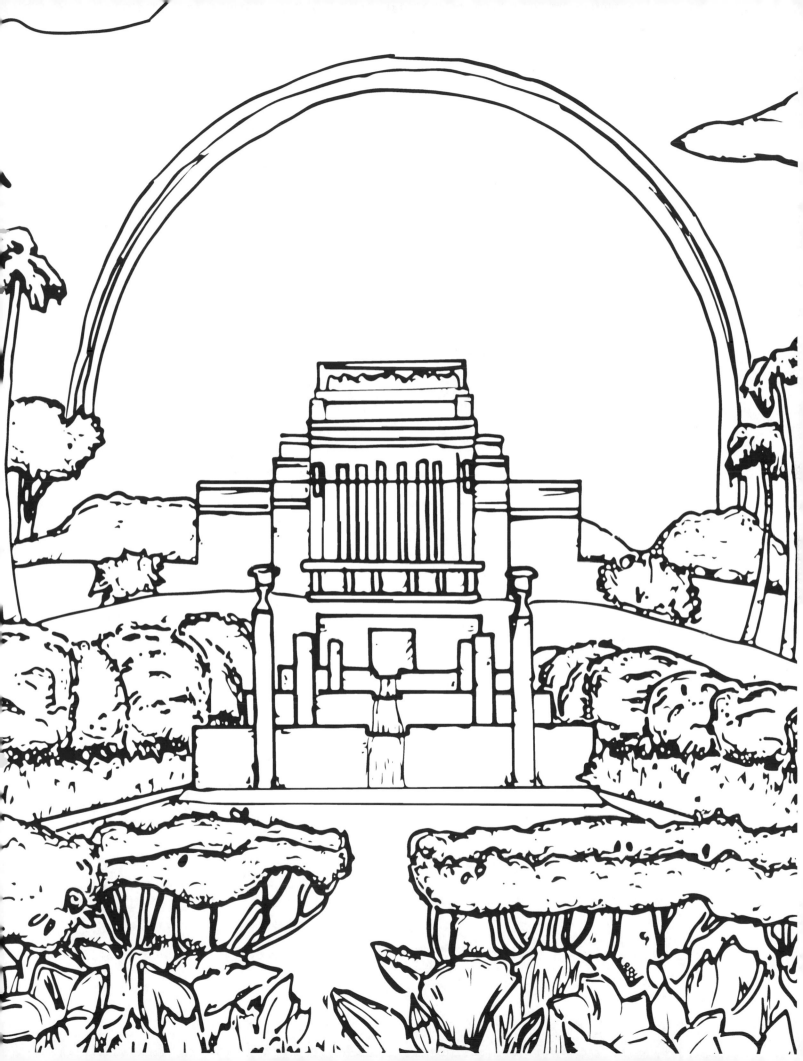

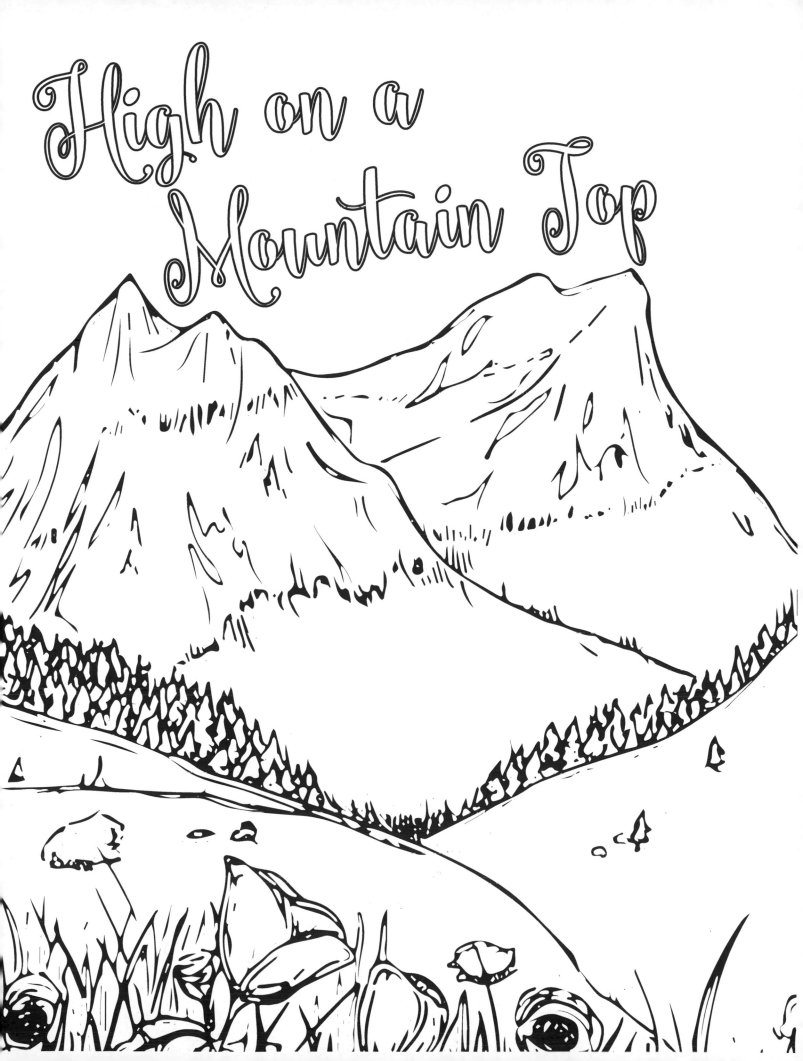

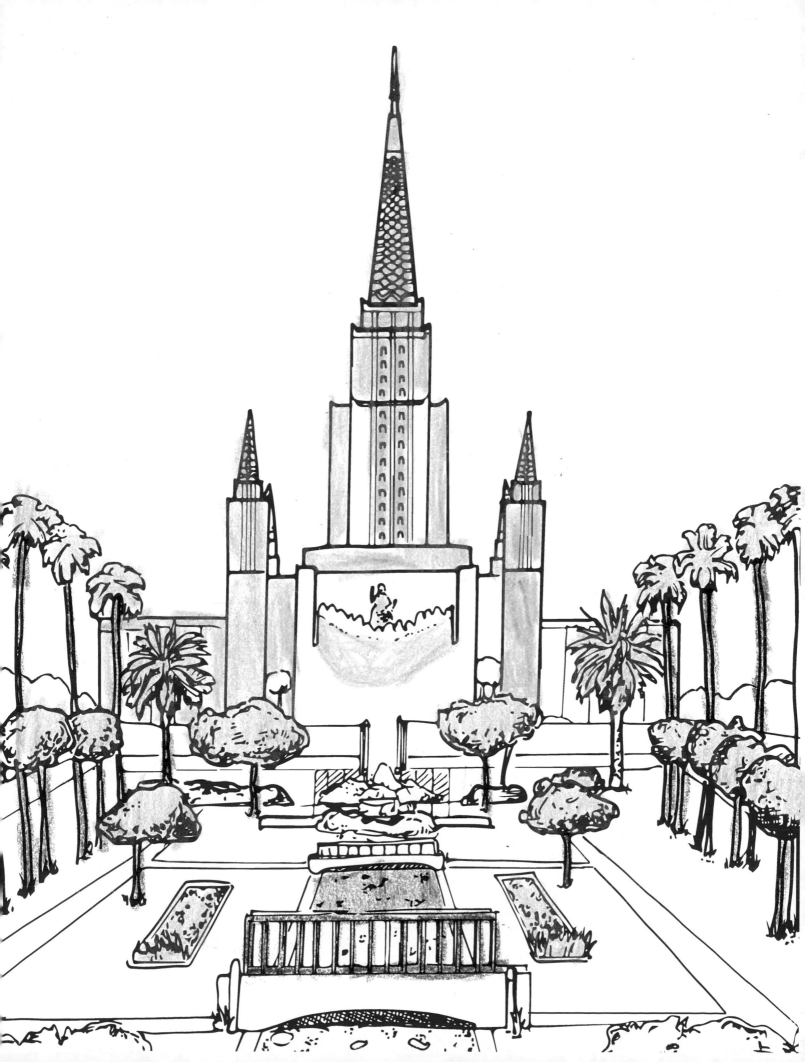

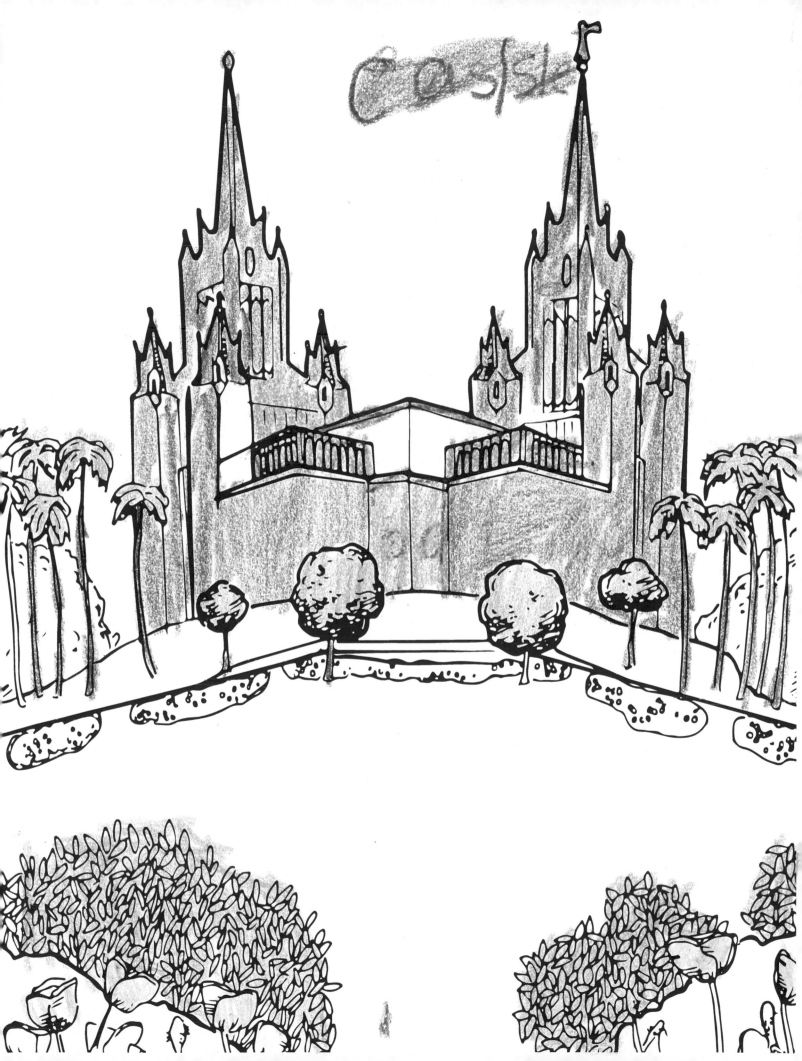

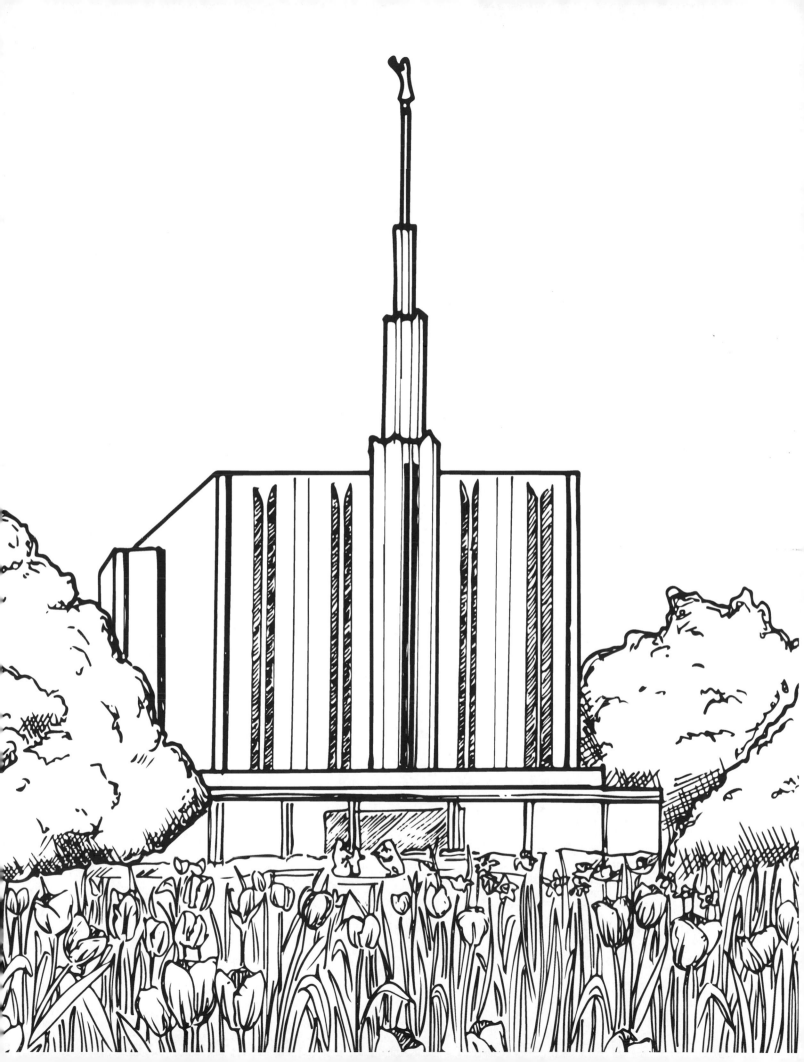

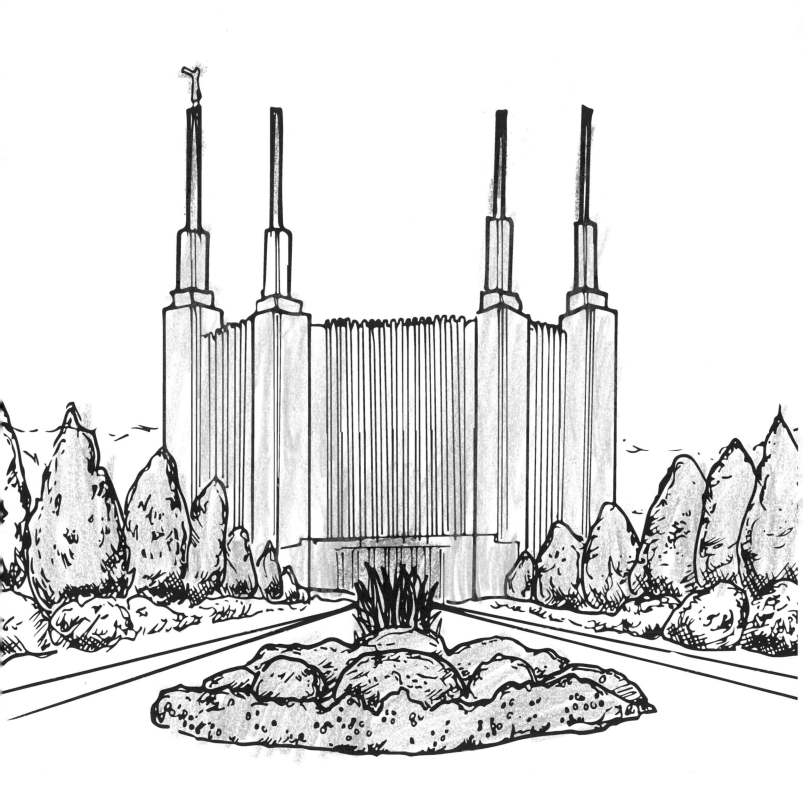

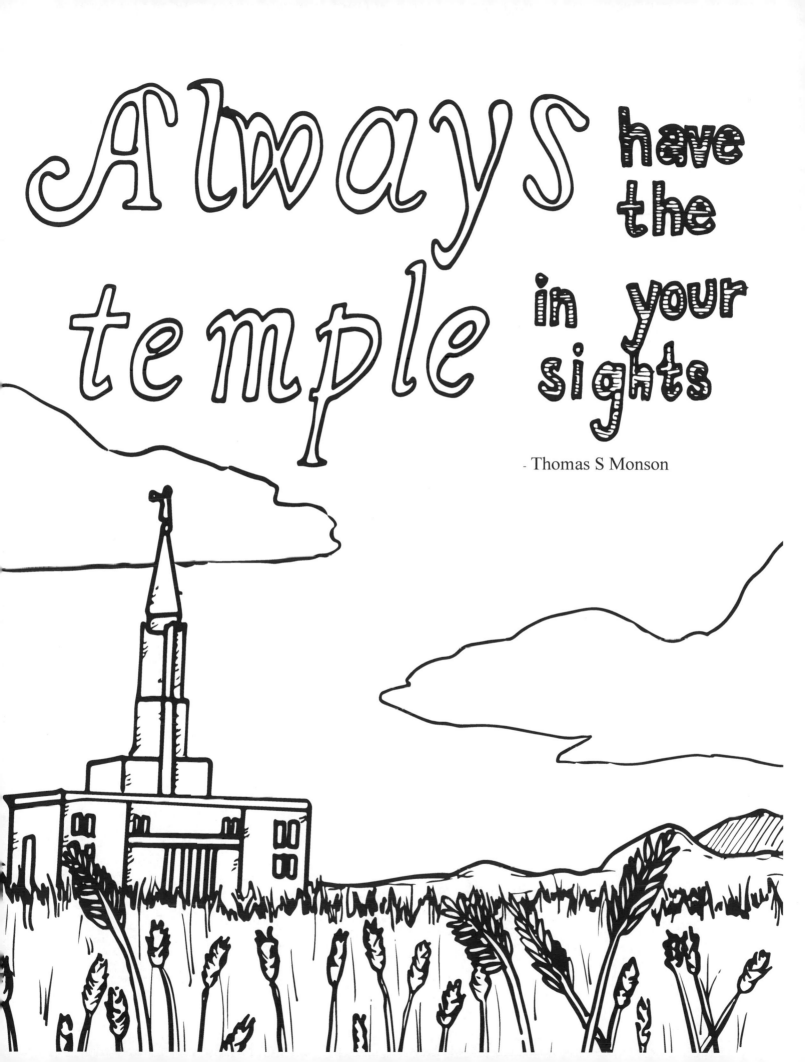

Always have the temple in your sights

- Thomas S Monson

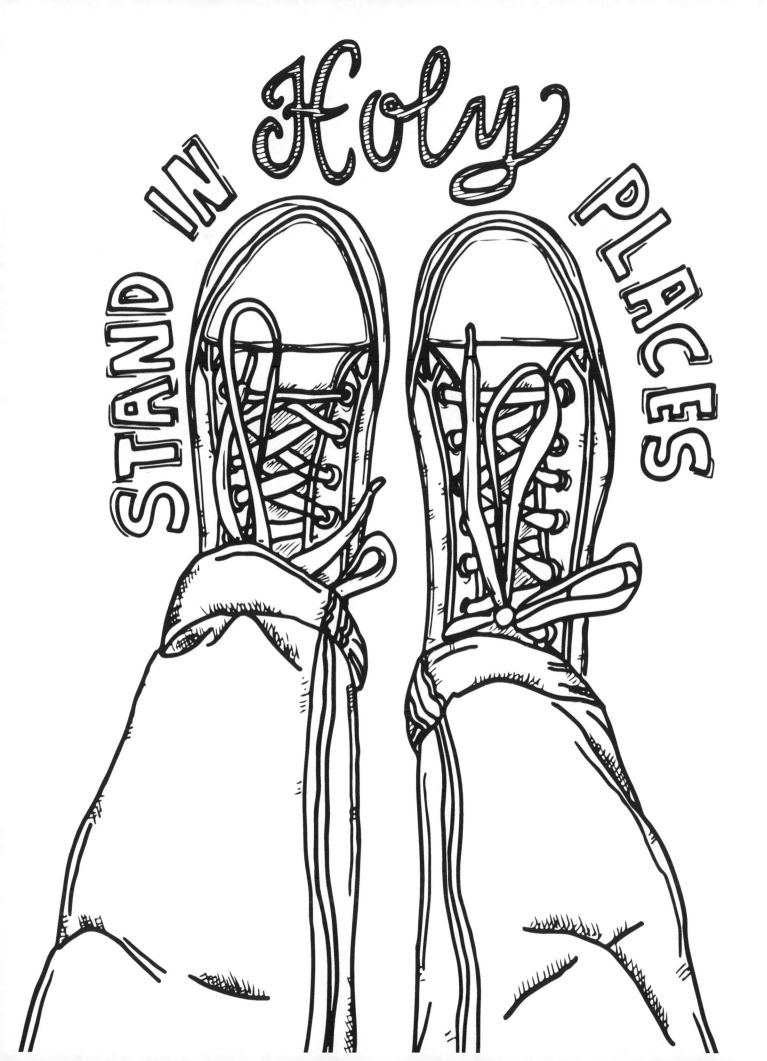

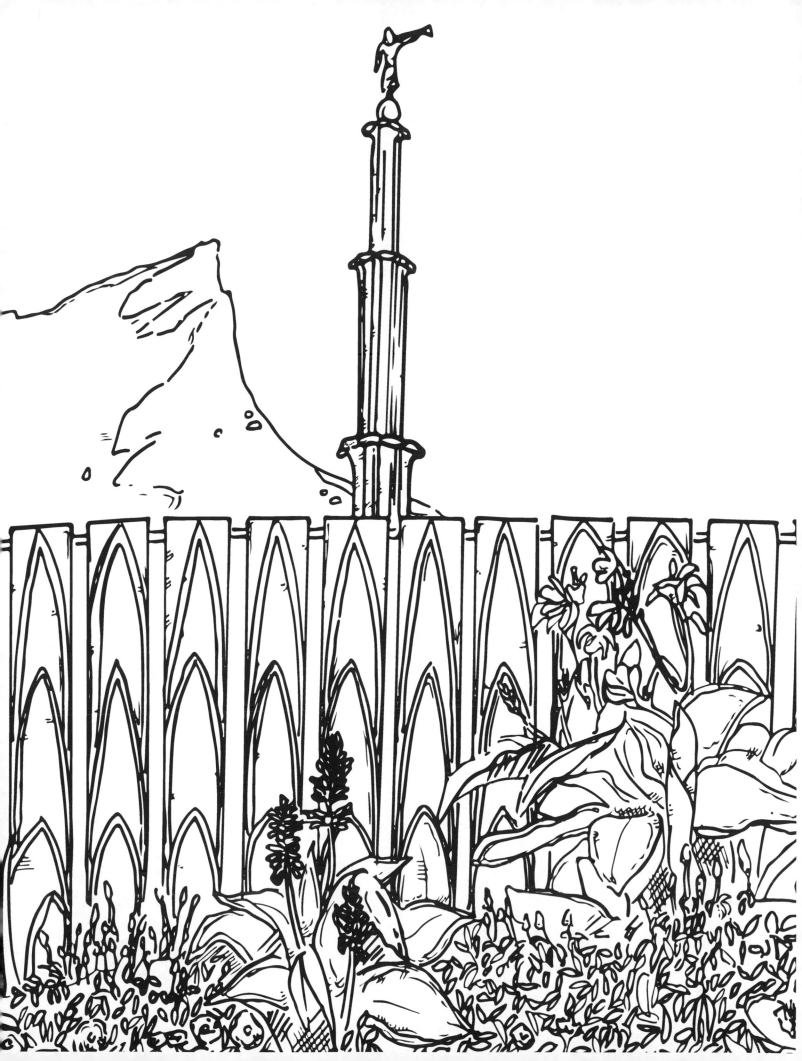

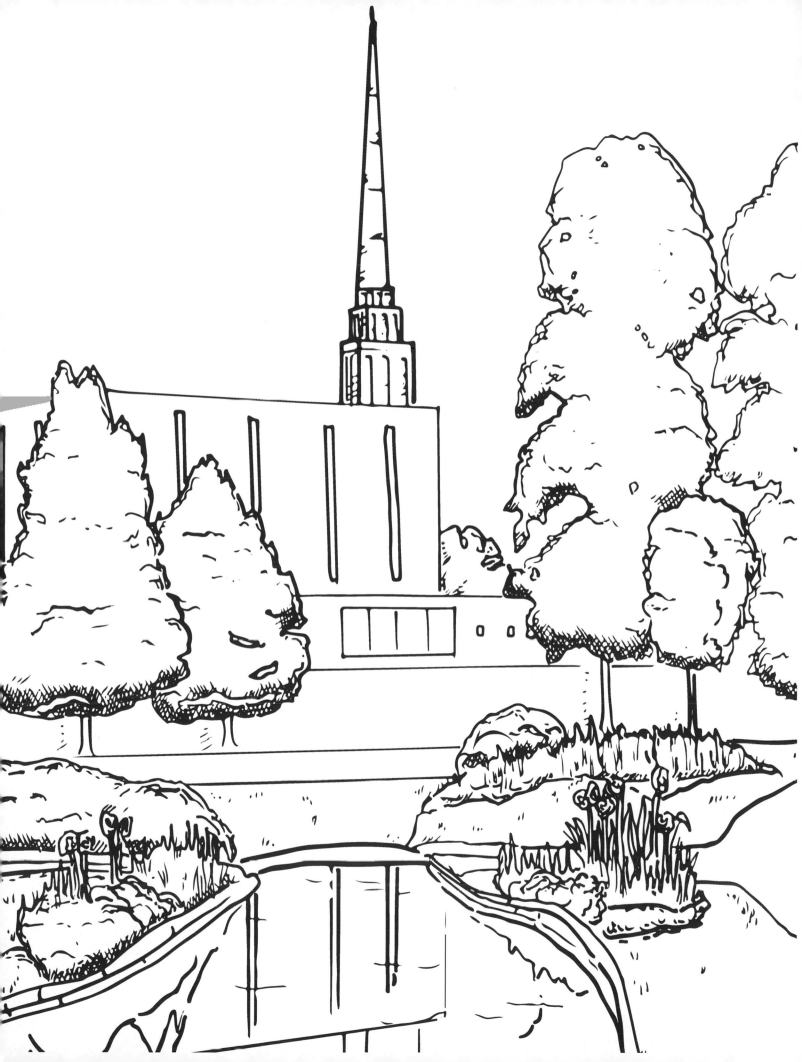

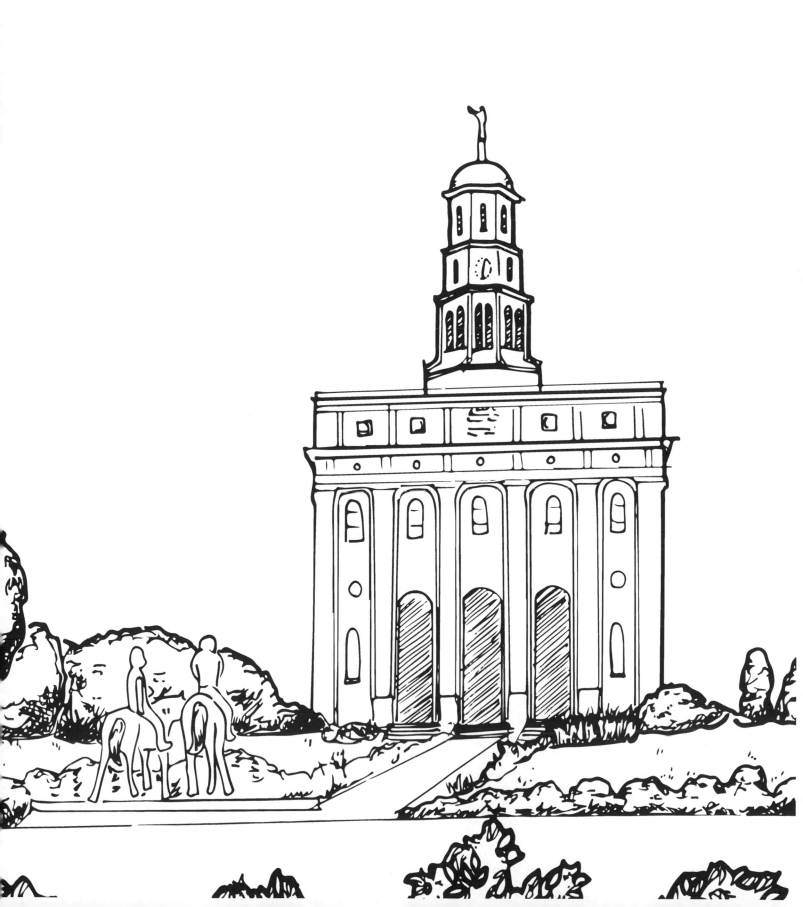

Angel Moroni Facts

"And I saw another angel fly in the midst of heaven, having the everlasting gospel to preach unto them that dwell on earth, and to every nation, and kindred, and tongue, and people."-Revelations 14:6

The Salt Lake Temple was the first Temple to add an upright Angel Moroni statue.

Fun Fact 1: Although most Angel Moroni statues face East, there are seven that do not.

Fun Fact 2: There are nine temples without an Angel Moroni at the top. Instead, these nine temples have either decorative spires or domes. These temples include: St. George Utah Temple, Logan Utah Temple, Manti Utah Temple, Laie Hawaii Temple, Cardston Alberta Temple, Mesa Arizona Temple, Hamilton New Zealand Temple, Oakland California Temple, and Paris France Temple.

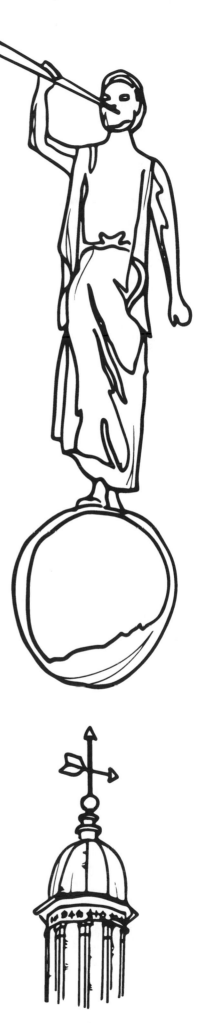

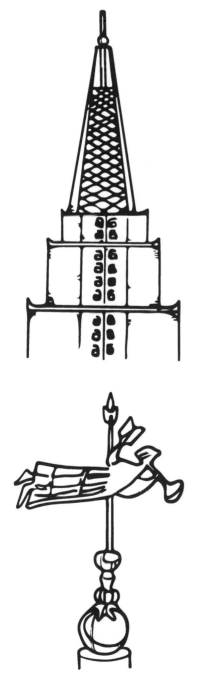

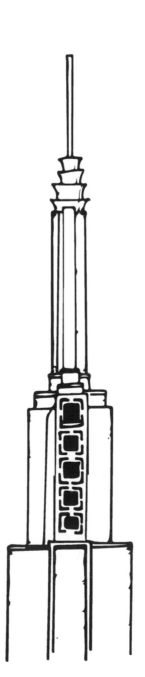

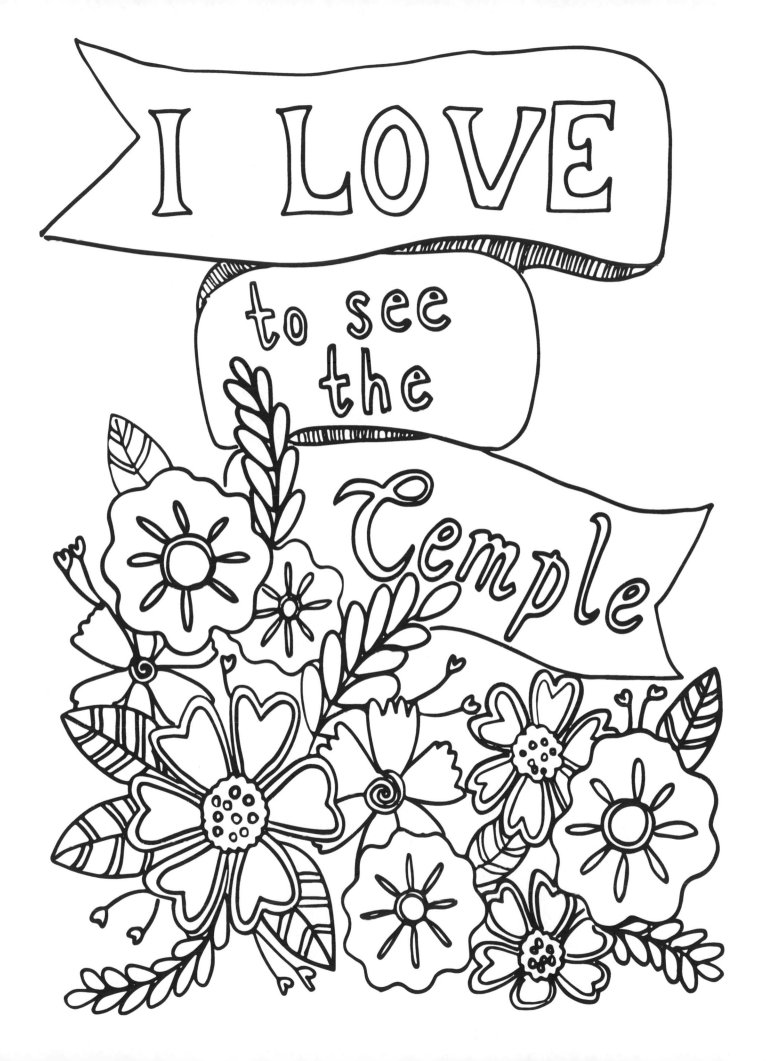

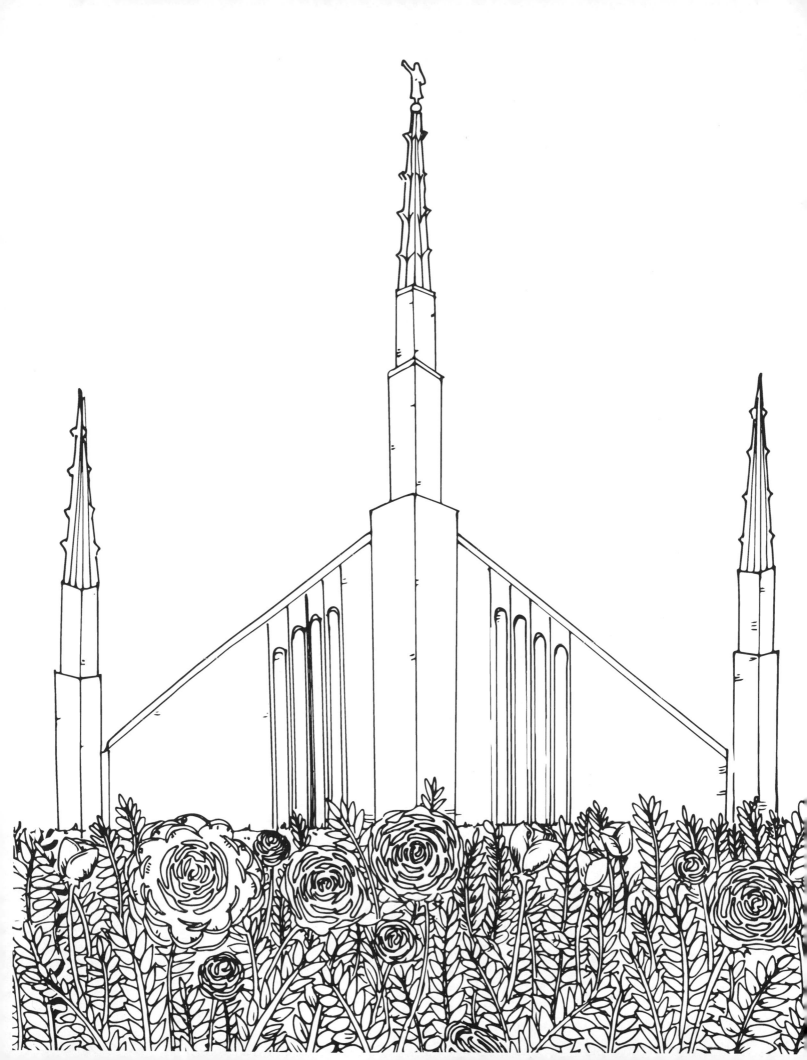

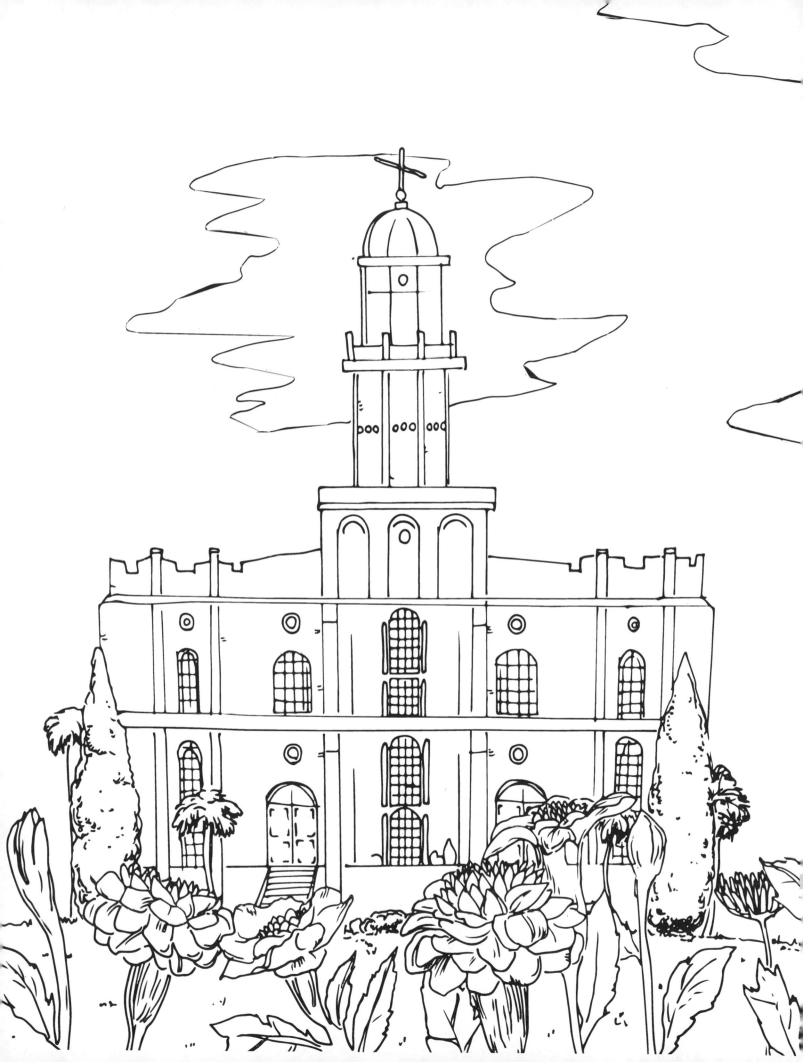

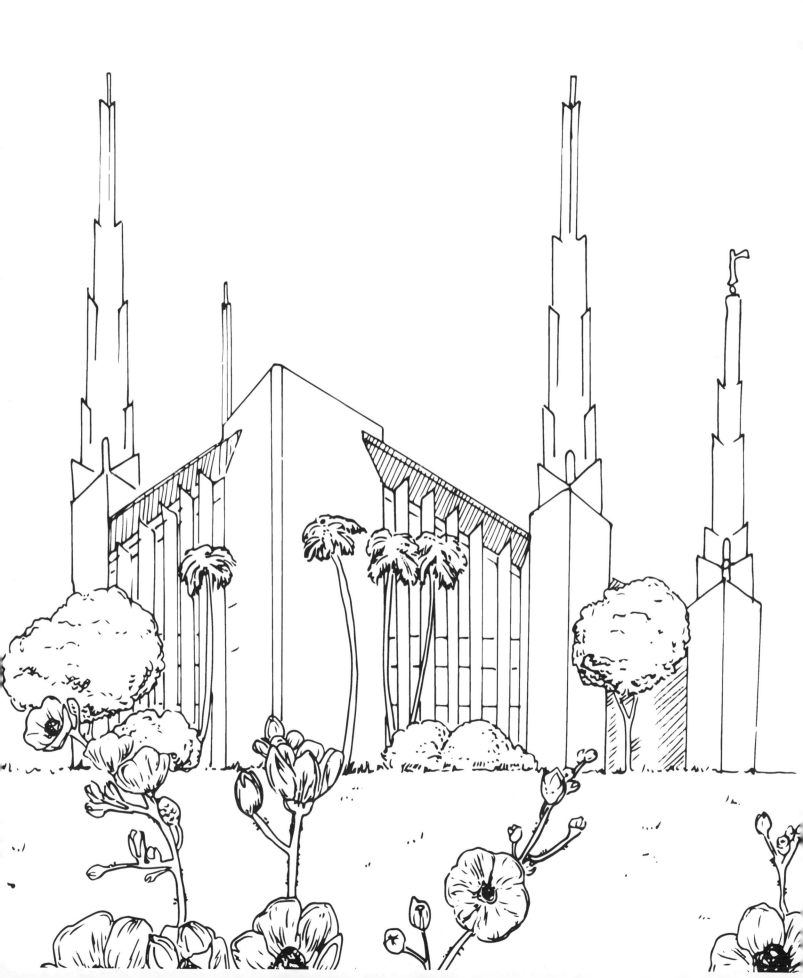

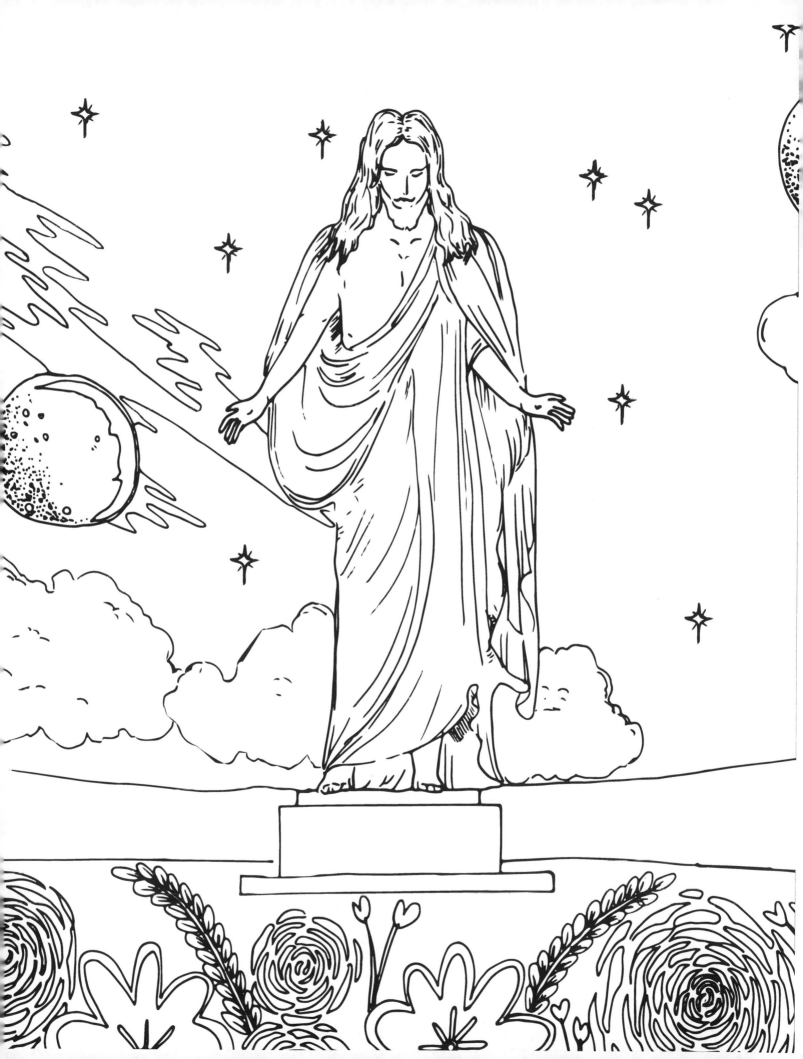

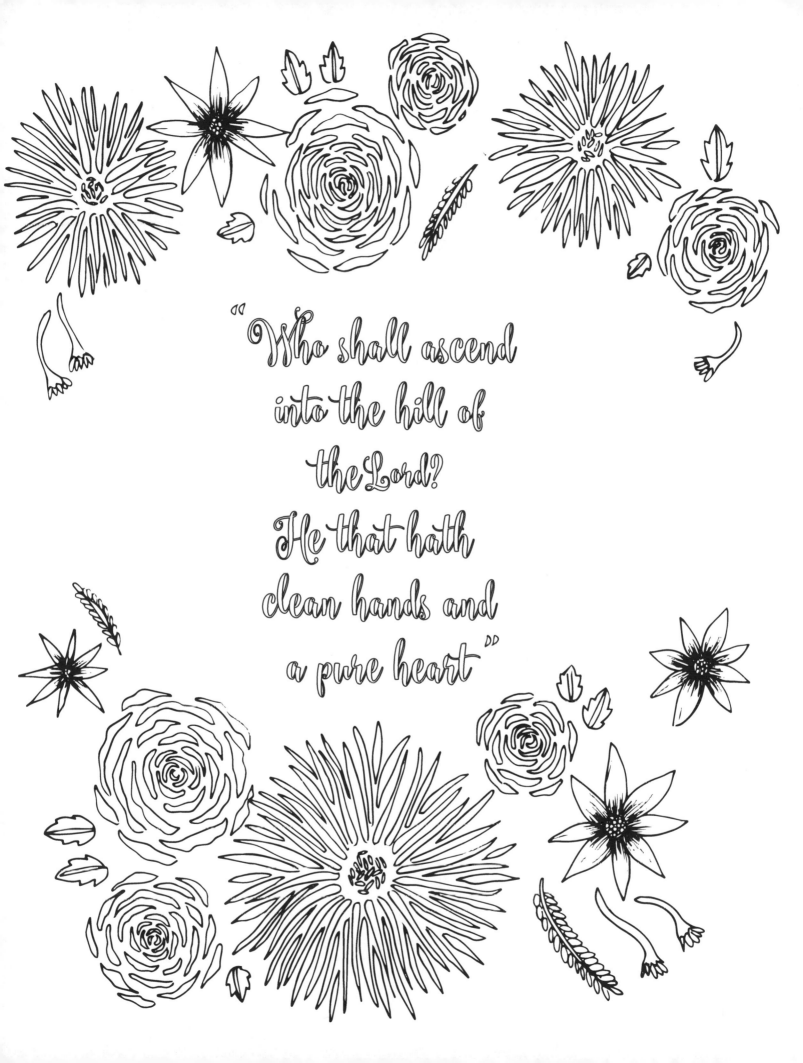

"Who shall ascend into the hill of the Lord? He that hath clean hands and a pure heart"

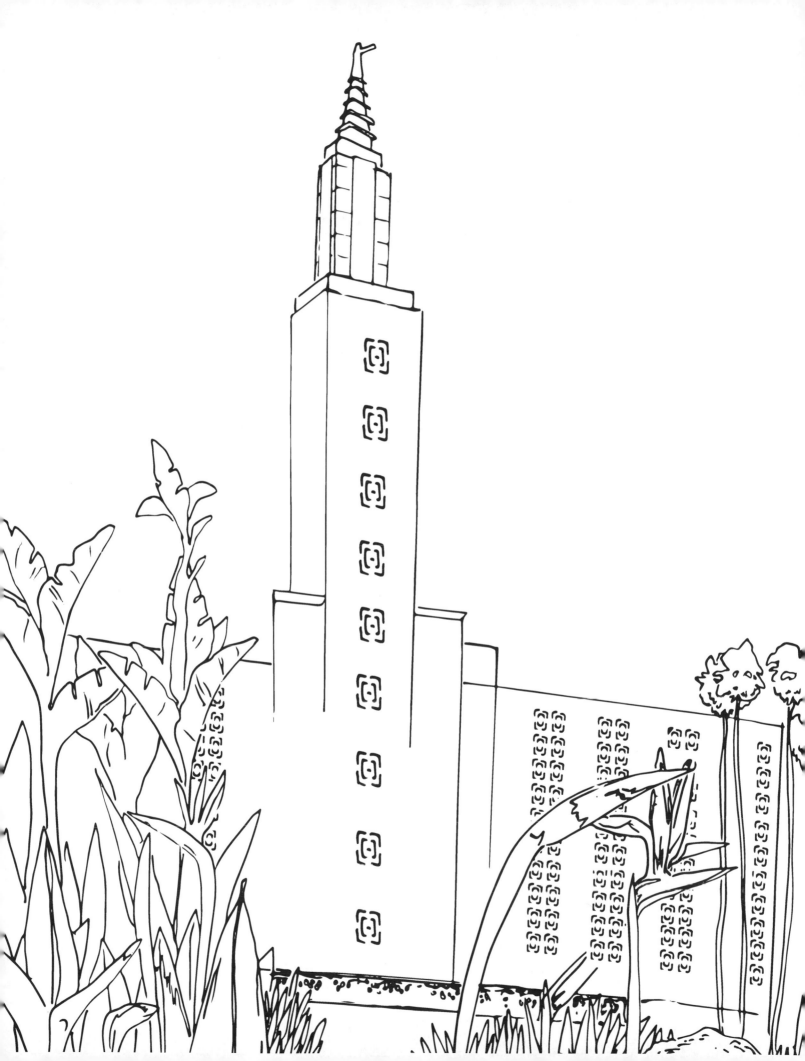

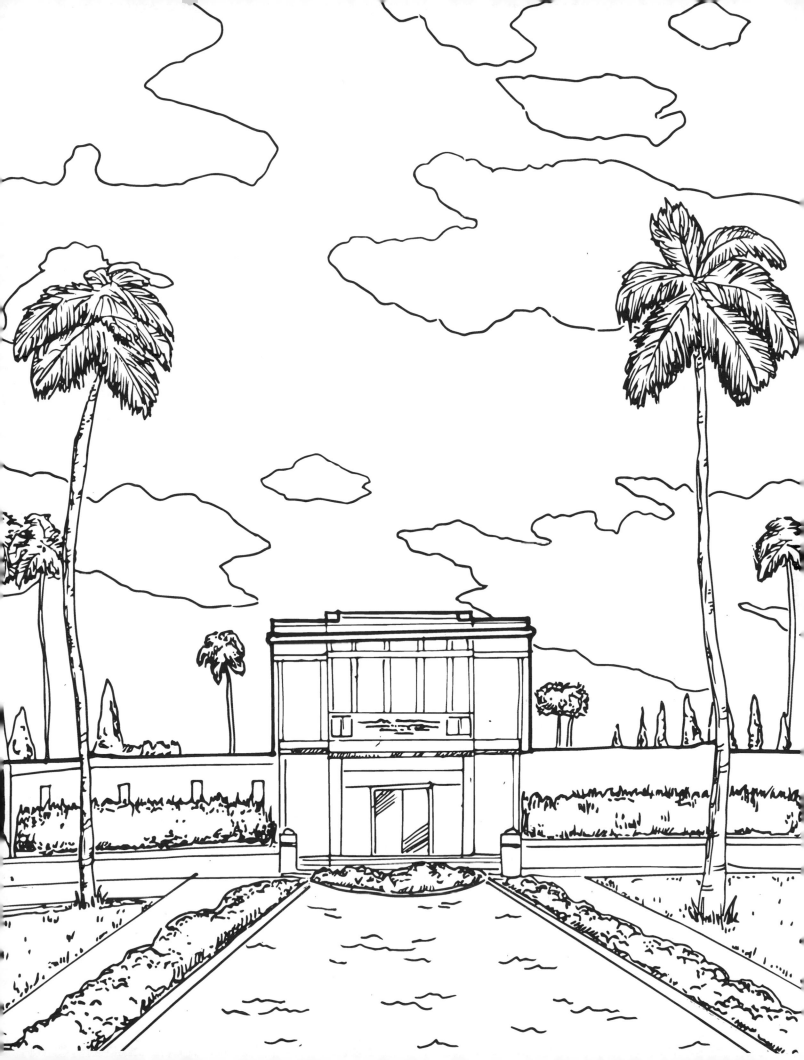

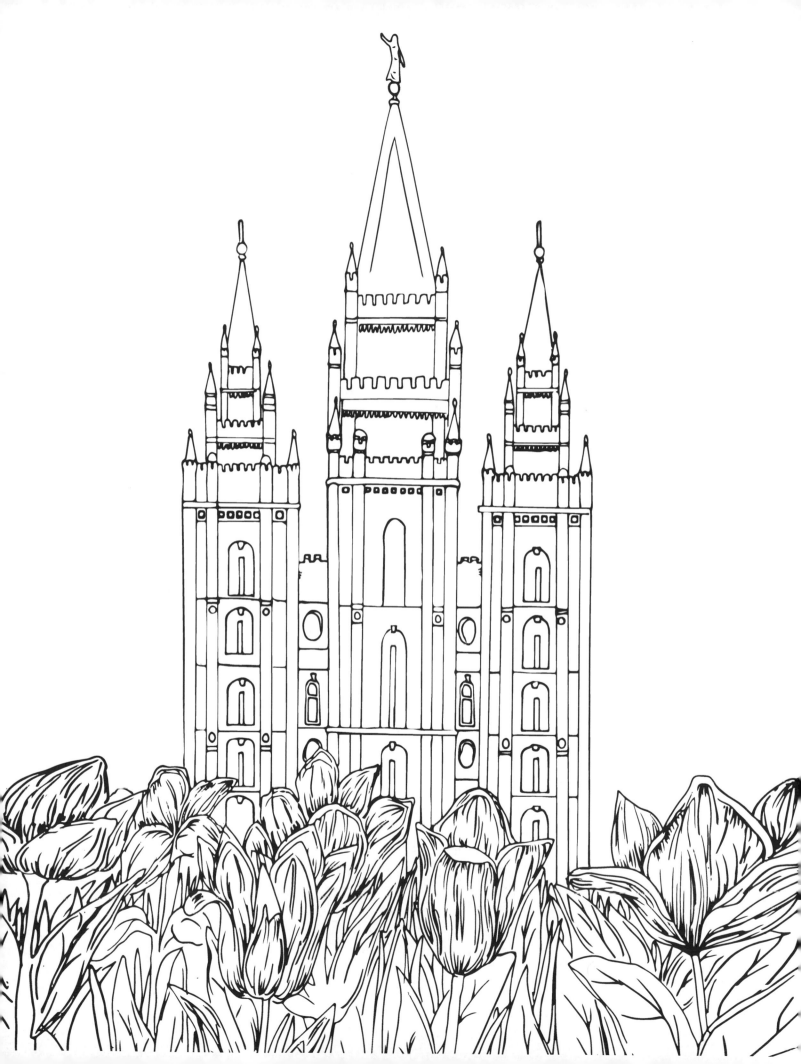

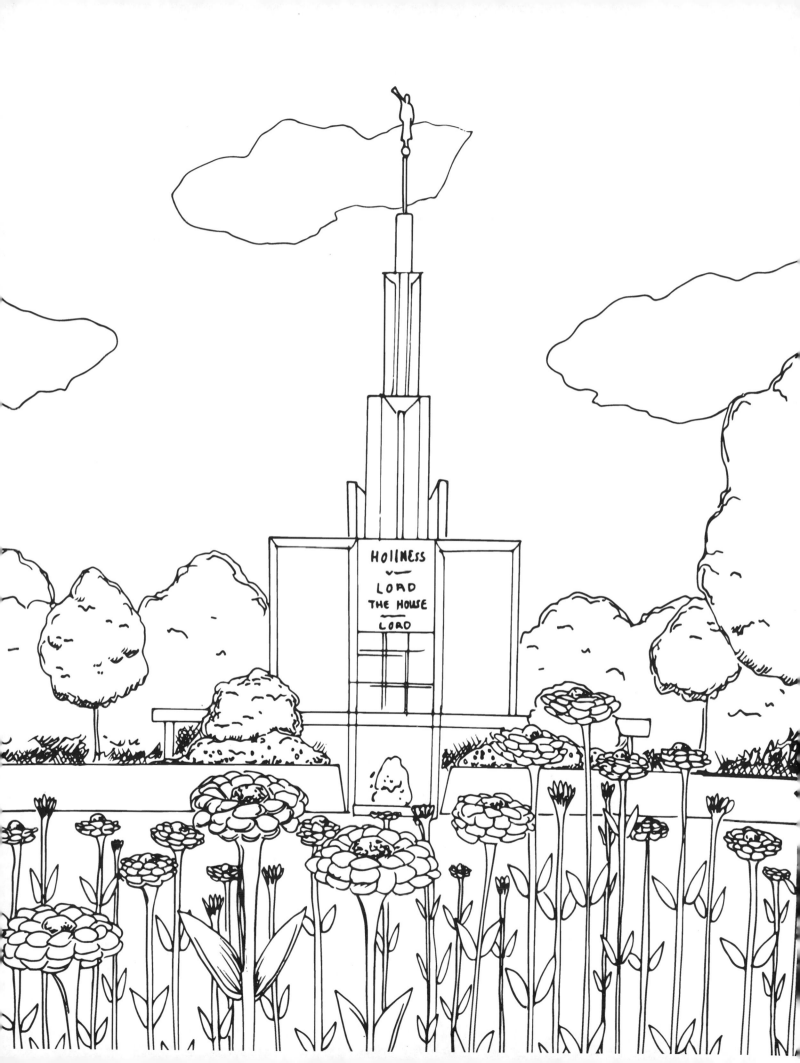

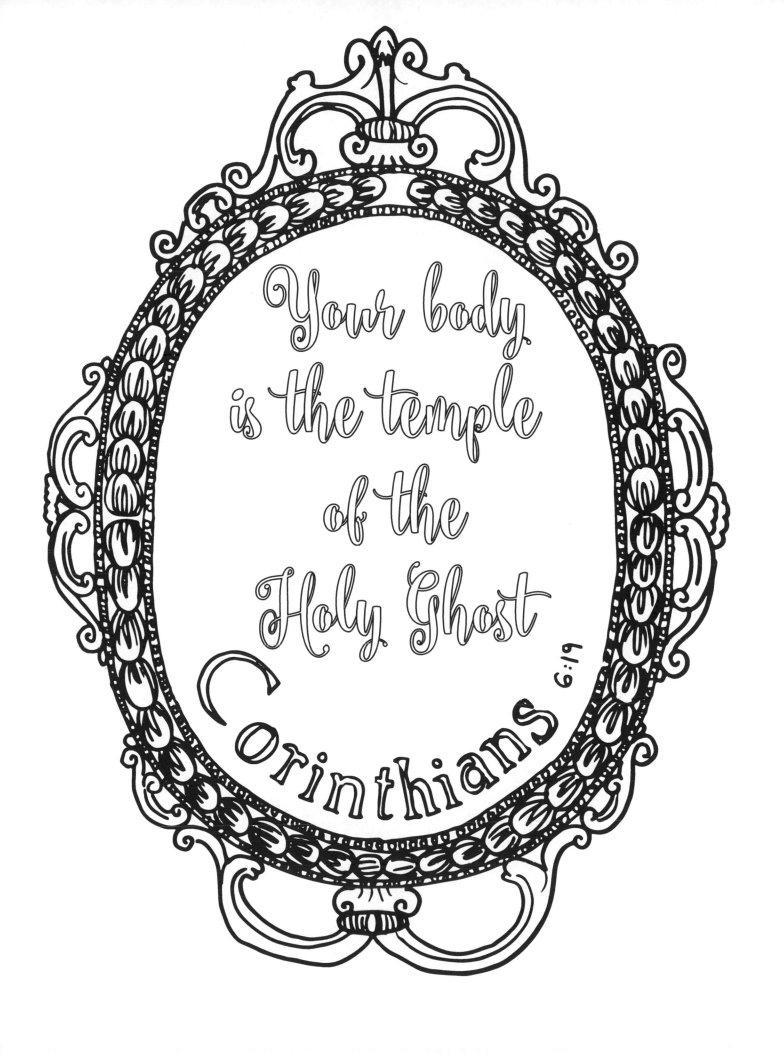

Your body is the temple of the Holy Ghost

Corinthians 6:19

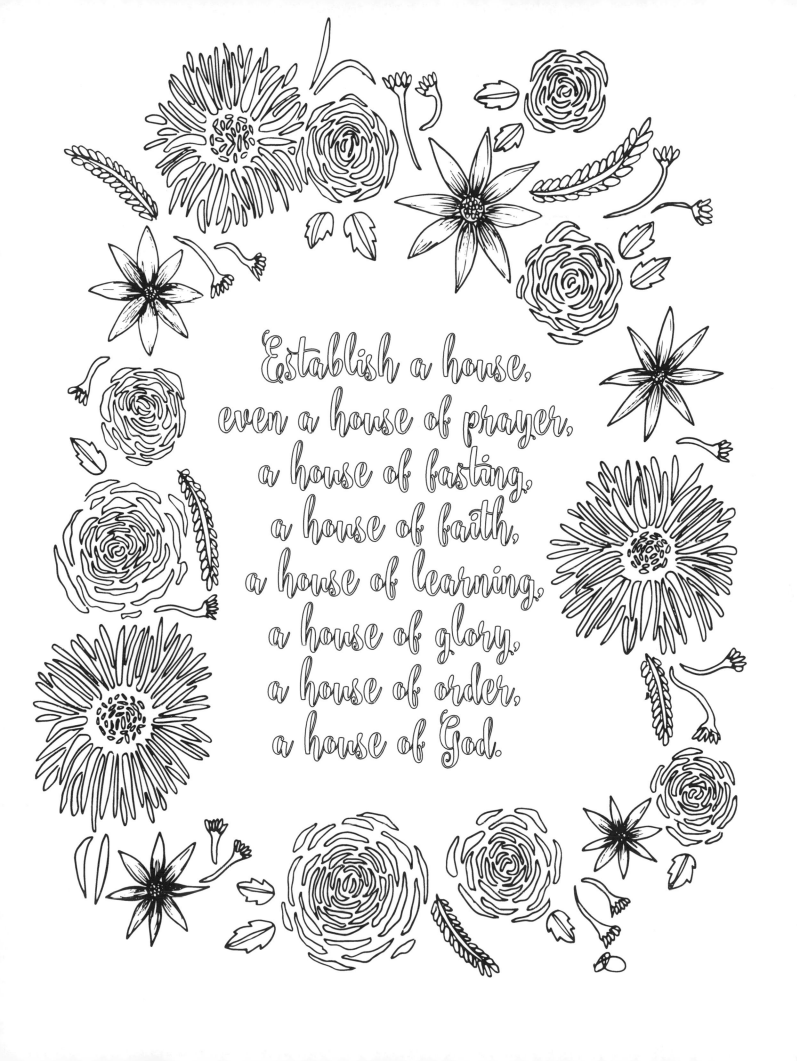

Establish a house,
even a house of prayer,
a house of fasting,
a house of faith,
a house of learning,
a house of glory,
a house of order,
a house of God.

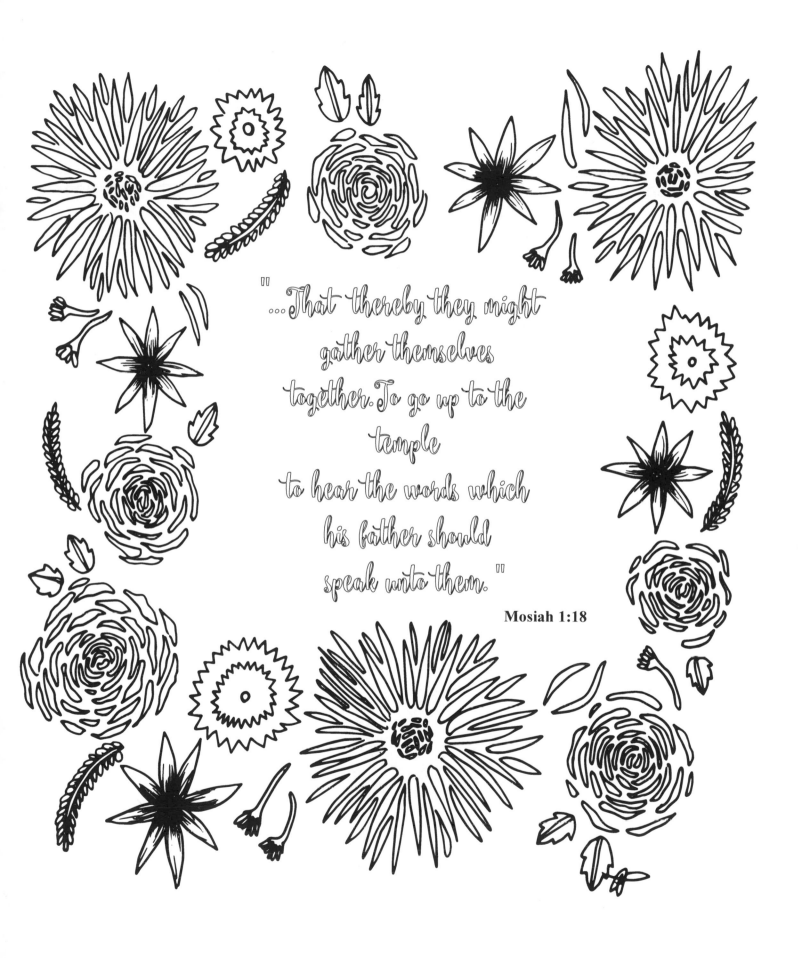

"...That thereby they might gather themselves together. To go up to the temple to hear the words which his father should speak unto them."

Mosiah 1:18

Temples Around the World

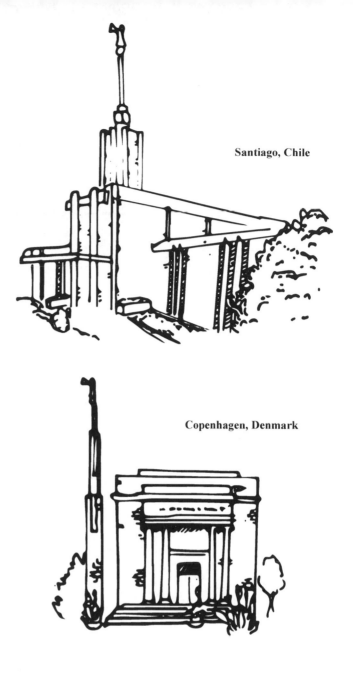

Santiago, Chile

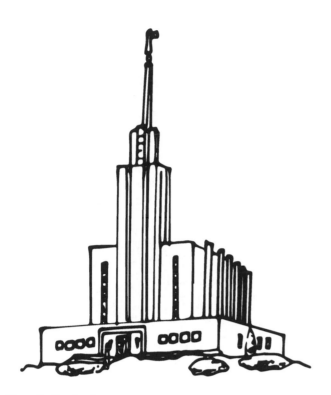

Bern, Switzerland

Copenhagen, Denmark

Hong Kong, China

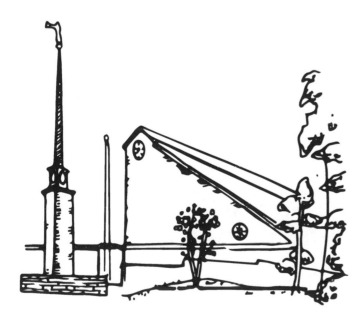

Stockholm, Sweden

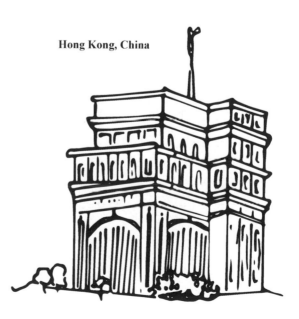

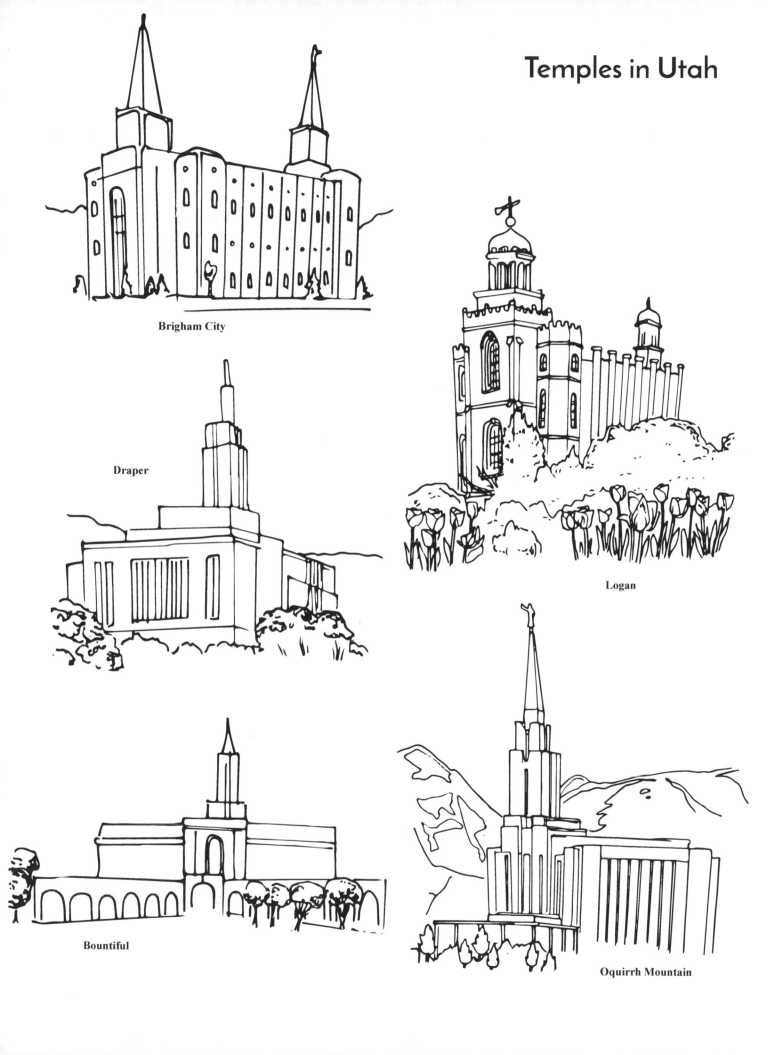

Temples in Utah

Brigham City

Draper

Logan

Bountiful

Oquirrh Mountain

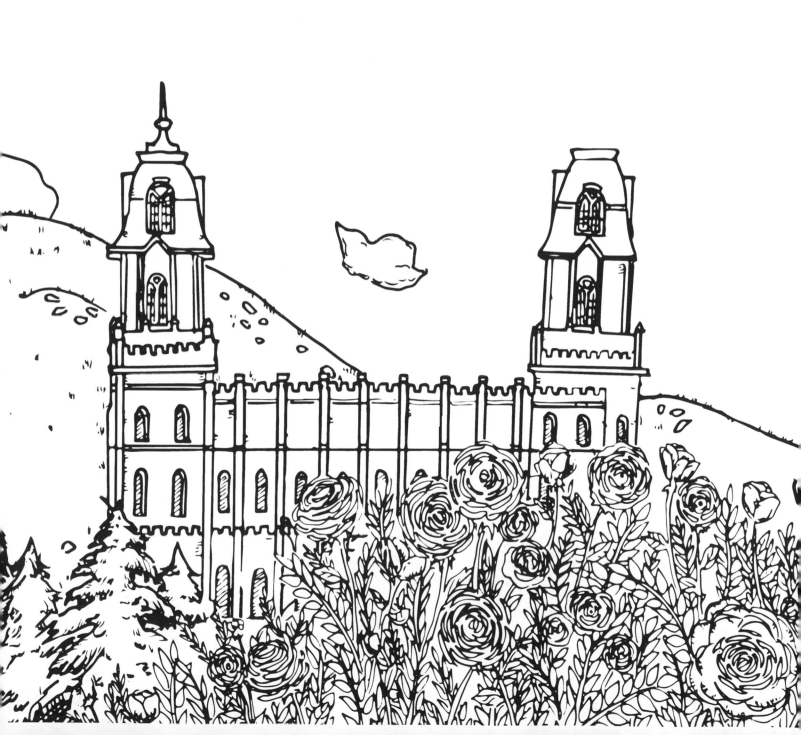